FROM SEA to SHINING SEA

CALIFORNIA

TERESA KENNEDY

Consultants

MELISSA N. MATUSEVICH, PH.D.
Curriculum and Instruction Specialist
Blacksburg, Virginia

LINDA COPPER
Librarian, San Marcos Middle School
San Marcos, California

CHILDREN'S PRESS®
A DIVISION OF SCHOLASTIC INC.

New York • Toronto • London • Auckland • Sydney • Mexico City
New Delhi • Hong Kong • Danbury, Connecticut

California is in the western part of
the United States. It is bordered by
Oregon, Nevada, Arizona, Mexico,
and the Pacific Ocean.

Project Editor: Meredith DeSousa
Art Director: Marie O'Neill
Photo Researcher: Marybeth Kavanagh
Design: Robin West, Ox and Company, Inc.
Page 6 map and recipe art: Susan Hunt Yule
All other maps: XNR Productions, Inc.

Library of Congress Cataloging-in-Publication Data
Kennedy, Teresa.
    California/ Teresa Kennedy.
        p. cm.—(From sea to shining sea)
    Includes bibliographical references (p.) and index.
    ISBN 0-516-22309-7
    1.California—Juvenile literature. [1. California.] I. Title. II. From sea to shining sea (Series)
F861.3 .K46 2001
979.4—dc21   00-069387

TABLE of CONTENTS

CHAPTER

ONE   Introducing the Golden State 4

TWO   The Land of California 7

THREE   California Through History 22

FOUR   Governing California 44

FIVE   The People and Places of California 54

California Almanac 70

Timeline 72

Gallery of Famous Californians 74

Glossary 75

For More Information 76

Index 77

INTRODUCING THE GOLDEN STATE

The Golden Gate Bridge is a well-known symbol of San Francisco.

California is a golden, magical place. California's nickname, the Golden State, comes from the days of the great American gold rush and also from the golden poppies that are the state flower. The name California comes from "California," the name of a magical land in a Spanish novel.

California is a magical place for the many people who come here to make their fortunes. Some people want to be movie stars in Hollywood, and others want to succeed in business or the computer industry. Many successful and important people in history came from California. Former President Richard Nixon was born in Yorba Linda, and the first female American astronaut, Dr. Sally Ride, was born in Los Angeles. California is also the birthplace of one of the world's most famous characters—Mickey Mouse! This free-spirited state has such a mix of culture, land, and industry that it continues to attract people from all around the world.

In fact, California is a state of great ethnic diversity. A great number of Hispanics, people from Mexico and Latin America, live in California. There are also many Asians, African-Americans, and some Native Americans living there. This variety of people and cultures is one of the many reasons people find the Golden State so appealing.

What comes to mind when you think of California?

- Giant redwood trees
- The Golden Gate Bridge
- Movie crews filming in Hollywood
- Computer and electronics companies creating new technology
- Hispanics, Asians, African-Americans, and Native Americans celebrating their culture
- Hiking the mountain trails at Mount Whitney and the Sierra Nevada
- Huge farms where grapes, artichokes, and oranges are grown
- Sunshine, palm trees, and the sandy beaches of the southern coast
- Early Native Americans and missionaries at the San Diego missions
- Coyotes and cacti in Death Valley
- Early Americans rushing to California in search of gold

The Golden State has something for everyone. Mountains and deserts, bustling cities and rich farmland, beautiful beaches for swimming, and wintry slopes for skiing. All this and more in just one state. What are you waiting for? Let's find out about California!

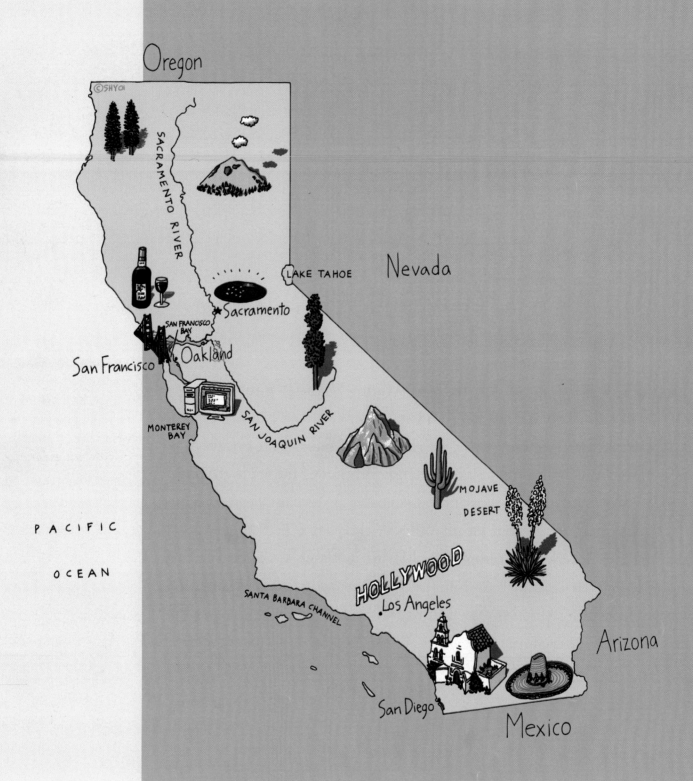

Oregon

©SHY01

SACRAMENTO RIVER

Nevada

LAKE TAHOE

Sacramento

SAN FRANCISCO
BAY

San Francisco

Oakland

MONTEREY
BAY

SAN JOAQUIN RIVER

PACIFIC

OCEAN

MOJAVE

DESERT

SANTA BARBARA CHANNEL

HOLLYWOOD

Los Angeles

Arizona

San Diego

Mexico

CHAPTER TWO

THE LAND OF CALIFORNIA

California is one of the biggest states in the entire country. It is smaller than only Alaska and Texas. California covers such a large area that it has a wide range of landscape, climate, and geography. You can ski in the mountains in the morning, and sunbathe on the beach in the afternoon! Northern California is very different from the southern part, where most people in the state live.

California is in the southwest corner of the United States. It is one of the Pacific Coast states. The western border of California is made up of the beautiful shores of the Pacific Ocean. Arizona and Nevada are located to the east, and Oregon is to the north. Mexico borders southern California.

A long line of cracks, or faults, in Earth's surface runs from southern to northern California. These cracks in the surface are the result of pieces of Earth's crust suddenly shifting. When these pieces of rock shift

The combination of climate and soil in Napa Valley make it the perfect place for growing grapes for wine. Today it is home to many successful wine producers.

The San Andreas Fault is about 700 miles long (1,120 km) and at least 10 miles (16 km) deep. Movement along the San Andreas Fault caused the great San Francisco earthquake in 1906.

and rub against each other, specifically along the fault line, the vibrations cause earthquakes. Sometimes Earth's crust moves very slightly and causes tremors that are so small they aren't felt by people. Other times it moves many feet in a few seconds, producing a large earthquake.

California has four main regions. They are the Coast, the Mountains, the Central Valley, and the Desert. The characteristics of these regions have a big effect on the lives of the people who live there.

THE COAST

California has 840 miles (1,352 kilometers) of coastline. Since it's such a long coastline, many people think of it in two sections—north and south. When people talk about the north coast, they are usually talking about the area north of San Francisco Bay. The south coast is south of the bay. The five largest cities in California can be found along the California coast.

The north coast has areas of real wilderness, where there are no paved roads and no towns. These areas tell us what California might have been like hundreds and hundreds of years ago. The northern area has a strong surf, a rocky coast, and thick forests. It is often covered in thick fog. Fog along the coast usually forms when warm, moist air meets the cold ocean water. Years ago, the north coast had lighthouses and foghorns to warn ships away from dangerous coastal waters. Today, ships have radar and sonar devices, so foghorns and lighthouses are no longer needed.

The southern coast has long, flat stretches of beach. The surf is gentle, and the water temperatures are warm. This makes the southern coast attractive to tourists and outdoor-sports fans.

Southern California's beaches are a popular place for sun-bathing, sailing, and wind-surfing.

California has two groups of islands located off its coast. The Channel Islands, sometimes called the Santa Barbara Islands, are a group of islands stretching about 150 miles (241 km) along the Southern California coast. The largest is Santa Cruz, at 98 square miles (254 sq km). Other islands in the group are Santa Catalina, San Miguel, Santa Rosa, Santa Barbara, and San Clemente. The islands themselves are rugged and rocky, and only two of them, Santa Cruz and Santa Catalina, have forests. Most of these islands have sea caves and are home to all kinds of distinctive plant life.

Santa Rosa Island is part of the Channel Islands National Park. The Channel Islands have many plant species that can't be found anywhere else in the world.

A smaller group of islands known as the Farallons lie off the coast of Northern California. Like the islands to the south, these are rugged and rocky. The Farallons total only about 211 acres (85 hectares), but they are home to an important national wildlife refuge and are protected habitats for many types of birds, sea lions, and sea otters.

THE MOUNTAINS

The western mountains of California are part of a group of mountains known as the Coastal Ranges. These mountains stretch from southern Alaska all the way down the California coast—some parts of the Coastal ranges lie under the waters of the Pacific Ocean! In Southern California are the Los Angeles ranges, which are small groups of mountains. Included in the Los Angeles ranges are the San Bernardino, San Gabriel, and San Jacinto mountains. Though not as high or rugged as some of the other mountain ranges in California, the Coastal Ranges are still very rich in natural resources such as oil and mineral deposits.

California also has volcanoes, though most of them haven't erupted since prehistoric times. Lassen Peak, located in the northcentral portion of the state, is still considered an active volcano.

In eastern California, you'll find the beautiful Sierra Nevada mountain ranges. The Sierra Nevada ranges stretch for 400 miles (644 km)

Climbing Mount Whitney is difficult, but 20,000 or more people reach the top every year.

along the state's eastern border. The highest point on the main continent of the United States is Mount Whitney in the Sierra Nevada. Mount Whitney rises 14,494 feet (4,418 meters) and is considered one

Giant sequoias are some of the largest living things around. They can grow up to 26 stories tall and are 20 and 30 feet in diameter.

of California's natural wonders. Gold was first discovered in the Sierra Nevada foothills on the western side. The Sierras are also home to Yosemite, Sequoia, and Kings Canyon national parks, as well as a number of national forest preserves and almost 1,000 lakes.

WHO'S WHO IN CALIFORNIA?

John Muir (1838–1914) was born in Scotland but played a big part in preserving California's wilderness. He is well known for his lone journeys in the Sierra Nevada. He was influential in getting Yosemite designated a national park.

THE CENTRAL VALLEY

The area that lies between the Sierra Nevada ranges in the east and the coastal ranges in the west is known as the Great Central Valley. The Central Valley stretches for 450 miles (724 km) north to south and fifty miles (80 km) east to west. It is divided into two sections—the Sacramento Valley in the northern part of the state and the San Joaquin Valley in the southern part of the state.

Both parts of the Central Valley are important for farming and agriculture. Good soil is only one of the reasons for the valley's success. The valley is mostly flat, making the land easy to farm. Also, California's mild weather offers a long growing season.

Many workers are employed on farms in the Central Valley.

The crops grown in the valley change as you move north to south. Trees are grown for lumber in the far north. The wetlands above Sacramento are good for growing rice. Further south, the climate is milder and good for growing fruits and nuts. In southern portions of the valley, you'll find crops such as citrus and cotton.

THE DESERT

(opposite)
Joshua trees may look eerie, but they provide habitat for birds, mammals, lizards, and insects.

Sand dunes appear throughout the Mojave Desert. These are mounds of loose sand grains that are shaped by the wind.

California is home to many deserts. The Mojave Desert is in the southern portion of the state. Death Valley is in the southeast, and Owens Valley is in the east, at the southern end of the Sierra Nevada. One-fourth of California's total land area is made up of desert.

The Mojave Desert is a hot, dry mountainous basin. It receives very little rain—less than 5 inches (13 centimeters) a year. However, Californians have figured out ways to bring water into this very dry area using

pipes from rivers and reservoirs. As a result, this desert area is now used to grow crops such as cotton, citrus, and flowers.

Not only does California have the second-highest point in the United States, it also has the lowest. Death Valley is the lowest point in the Western hemisphere at 282 feet (86 m) below sea level. *Sea level* refers to the average level of the water in the ocean, between high and low tides. Death Valley has some of the highest temperatures ever recorded—134° Fahrenheit (57° Celsius)—and often the thermometer registers over 100°F (38°C). In spite of the heat, Death Valley is home to all kinds of wildlife, including foxes, coyotes, roadrunners, and reptiles of all kinds. Many plants also grow there, including yucca, cactus, sagebrush, wildflowers, and mesquite.

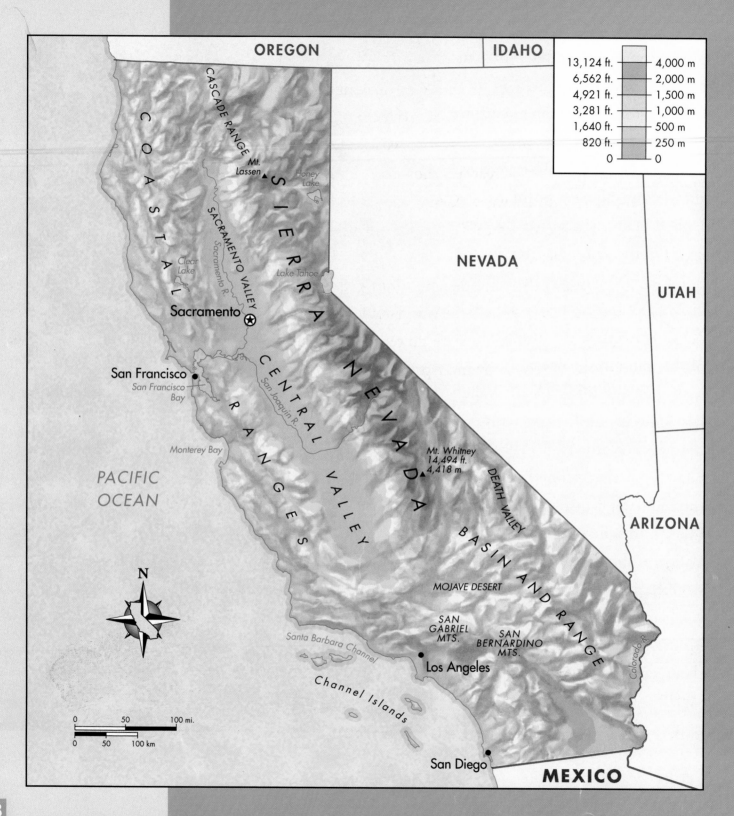

OREGON

IDAHO

13,124 ft. — 4,000 m
6,562 ft. — 2,000 m
4,921 ft. — 1,500 m
3,281 ft. — 1,000 m
1,640 ft. — 500 m
820 ft. — 250 m
0 — 0

CASCADE RANGE

Mt. Lassen ▲

Honey Lake

S I E R R A

Clear Lake

Sacramento R.

SACRAMENTO VALLEY

Lake Tahoe

NEVADA

Sacramento ✪

UTAH

C O A S T A L

San Francisco ●

San Francisco Bay

C E N T R A L

San Joaquin R.

N E V A D A

Monterey Bay

R A N G E S

V A L L E Y

Mt. Whitney
14,494 ft.
4,418 m ▲

PACIFIC
OCEAN

DEATH VALLEY

BASIN AND RANGE

MOJAVE DESERT

N

Santa Barbara Channel

SAN
GABRIEL
MTS.

SAN
BERNARDINO
MTS.

Colorado R.

ARIZONA

Los Angeles ●

Channel Islands

0   50   100 mi.
0   50   100 km

San Diego ●

MEXICO

Owens Valley, in the east, has canyons and hot springs—small streams of warm water flowing from the earth. Giant boulders and towering rock formations called mesas are evidence of the earth's changes over time. We can learn about the earth's age by studying layers of rock and minerals. Fossils of sea creatures show that, at one time, this desert area was completely under water. Gem deposits show that earthquakes caused parts of these rocks to be pushed up with great force from beneath the earth's surface.

Long-living trees called bristlecone pines grow in Owens Valley. They are considered to be one of the world's oldest living things—some are almost 5,000 years old! The state flower, the golden poppy, grows wild here and blooms in March and April.

RIVERS, LAKES, AND BAYS

The Sacramento River is the Golden State's longest river. It flows south through the Central Valley for 307 miles (494 km). It is so long that it is often referred to in sections, as the Upper and Lower Sacramento. The Sacramento River forms a large delta with the San Joaquin River. The San Joaquin is 368 miles (592 km) long and flows in a southwest direction. Both rivers meet northeast of San Francisco and drain into the San Francisco Bay.

The most important river in California is the Colorado River, which runs along the eastern border between California and Arizona. Water from this river is used in irrigation and reservoir systems throughout

Southern California where there is little rainfall. Because of irrigation, it is possible to farm areas where crops would not normally grow. Reservoirs make sure that cities in Southern California have a good water supply.

Other rivers in California are the Owens, Kern, Salinas, and Feather Rivers. In the spring, snow from Mount Whitney and the Sierra Nevada drain into the Kern, Kings, Tulare, and Kaweah Rivers. The Kern, in particular, is a popular place for whitewater rafting because it is both scenic and wild.

There are thousands of lakes in the state of California, mostly in the mountain ranges. The largest lake in California, the Salton Sea, was created when the Colorado River flooded in the early 1900s, bursting out of its manmade irrigation canal. The Colorado River flooded the valley for two years before it could be controlled. The Salton Sea is about 300 square miles (777 sq km) in size.

Lake Tahoe is a famous resort and recreational area. At 1,640 feet (500 m) it is also California's deepest lake. Other important lakes in California are Clear Lake, Eagle Lake, Honey Lake, and Shasta Lake. They are all in the northern part of the state.

San Francisco Bay lies just off the coast of San Francisco. Many

Skiers know that Lake Tahoe is a hot spot for some of the best skiing in the western United States.

people enjoy fishing, windsurfing, sailing, and swimming in San Francisco Bay. The San Diego Bay, in Southern California, serves as a home port to a commercial fishing fleet. It is also the headquarters of the 11th U.S. Naval District.

CLIMATE

Throughout California there are many differences in climate and temperature. In the mountains, there are heavy snows and cold temperatures. The coastline areas tend to have milder temperatures. The Central Valley has wide variations in both temperature and humidity, and Southern California tends to be hot and dry all year.

The desert areas of the state have extremes of hot and cold temperatures. In Death Valley, daytime temperatures often rise above 100°F (38°C) and nighttime temperatures fall to 0°F (-18°C).

In the summer and fall, Southern California gets hot, dry gusts of wind called the Santa Ana winds. These winds blow up to 60 miles per hour (that's as fast as a car drives on the highway)! California's mountain ranges increase the force of these winds. As the breezes are forced through narrow mountain canyons, the winds pick up speed. The Santa Ana winds often fuel the raging brush fires that threaten California's property and wildlife.

CHAPTER THREE

CALIFORNIA THROUGH HISTORY

Mission San Juan Bautista was founded in 1797. It sits right on the San Andreas fault. In the past it caused such shaking that the missionaries slept outside!

The year 2000 marked California's 150th birthday as a state. However, its history reaches centuries into the past. People lived in California more than 12,000 years ago. Most scientists believe that California's earliest Native Americans came from Asia. Paintings on cave walls and houses dug into the sides of cliffs give us a clue as to what they might have been like.

Some of the groups living in California were the Yokuts, the Maidu, the Miwok, and the Pomo. The Pomo were especially skilled at making baskets and decorating them with beads, feathers, and shells. The Maidu lived in small villages clustered around larger, more populated central villages. Other groups at this time included the Karok, the Mojave, the

EXTRA! EXTRA!

Similar to a state animal and a state flower, California was the first state to have an official state prehistoric artifact—an object produced by human hands that is proof of an earlier culture. In 1985 a small stone object carved in the shape of a bear was found in San Diego County. Scientists believe it was made by California's earliest people, 7000–8,000 years ago. It may have been created for religious use.

Paiute, and the Modoc. Some experts believe that California's natives spoke as many as 135 languages.

At that time, California was separated from the rest of the country by mountain ranges. As a result, the tribes who lived in California were very different from Native Americans elsewhere in the country. They had different languages, customs, and traditions. Geography also separated them from each other, which meant that there was very little war. They lived a peaceful existence, harvesting fruit, gathering nuts, and fishing from the streams. The acorn became especially important to their daily diet because of nearby oak trees that produced a plentiful supply of acorns.

The Paiute people were spread over central and southeastern California. They were known for their artistic baskets, which were specially treated for carrying water.

More recently, tribes that lived in California included the Hupa, the Shasta, the Chumash, the Cuahilla, and the Yuma nations. Many of these Native Americans were very important in helping the Spanish people who first came to California. They played a big role in the state's settlement, history, and growth.

One of the first explorers in this area was Juan Rodríguez Cabrillo. In 1542 he sailed from New Spain and discovered and named San Diego Bay and Santa Barbara. However, Spain did not make any claims on the area at that time.

In 1577, Sir Francis Drake, an explorer from England, set out on a voyage that would take him around the world in three years. Two years after

Sir Francis Drake sailed around the world in three years. He arrived in California in 1579.

setting off in 1579, Drake anchored his ship, the *Golden Hind*, just outside of what is now San Francisco. He claimed the area for England's Queen Elizabeth I and named it New Albion. Twenty-three years later, in 1602, Sebastián Vizcaíno explored the California coast around Monterey. Neither of these explorations led to settlements. California was difficult to reach by both land and sea, and people may have felt that a colony in this location would be cut off from the rest of the world.

Things changed in 1769, when Spaniards Gaspar de Portolá and Father Junípero Serra sailed from Mexico. They claimed the land for Spain and established a settlement at San Diego. Father Serra built missions, groups of buildings that included a fort and a church, as well as houses, farm buildings, and a school. Native Americans helped build the missions, and in exchange, Spanish missionaries taught them about farming. The real purpose of the missions, however, was to convert the native people of California to the Catholic religion. These early mission settlements were the beginning of a whole new way of life in California.

Spanish priests ran missions, where they hoped to convert Native Americans to Christianity.

From 1769 until 1823, twenty-one missions were built along what is known as the Camino Real, or "Royal Road" in Spanish. Although Native Americans were forced to help build the mission settlements, they were not given the buildings they built or the lands they farmed. They lived in huts surrounding the missions. However, the priests did not own the missions, either—they were controlled by the government of Spain. Many Native Americans stayed at the missions, tending the crops and herding cattle. Others fell victim to diseases such as smallpox and pneumonia.

In 1821 Mexico became independent from Spain. As a result, California was now ruled by Mexico, but the Mexican government paid little attention to its new territory. However, the Mexican government did give out huge land grants in the area of what is now Los Angeles, as long as people promised to stay for at least ten years. Ranches and farms were built, and the missions were disbanded. During this time, a new industry was discovered in California—beaver fur. Trappers came to California to hunt beavers and sell their fur.

It was about this time that people in the United States began to believe that their country should include all the lands between the Atlantic and the Pacific. Explorers from the east made their way to California, hearing tales of adventure and fortune. Tens of thousands of pioneers made the journey into California in the 1840s, but as it turned out, this was just the beginning.

Inspired by books and newspapers, Americans made their way west looking for adventure. They were excited by the prospect of making their fortunes and discovering greater freedom and rich farmlands. Many of these pioneers had emigrated from Europe and wanted to stake their claims in a new land. Almost all Americans thought the territories of California and Texas should become part of the United States rather than remain under Mexican rule. Tensions mounted between the United States and Mexico.

Although he wasn't a soldier, John C. Frémont led a small rebellion that ultimately gave California freedom from Mexico.

At the same time, John Charles Frémont, a mapmaker and explorer, arrived in California. Although his job was to make maps of the west, Frémont helped greatly to stir up support for the area's freedom. In 1846 American settlers in California started a small revolution and put themselves under Frémont's protection. A short time later, the Americans declared independence from Mexico and raised a flag showing a star and a grizzly bear. It was a major victory, and Frémont was a hero— The Bear Republic was born.

The United States was already fighting with Mexico for control of Texas when California settlers won their own freedom from Mexico in the Bear Flag Revolt.

Today, the state flag of California is modeled after the same flag that those early rebels used.

When the war with Mexico ended in 1848, California, like Texas, became a territory of the United States. It would be two more years before California became a state. What happened in those two years proved to be one of the most exciting times in California history.

"GOLD ON THE AMERICAN RIVER!"

In the late 1840s, many men in California worked for John Sutter, a Swiss immigrant who owned land and property around the area that is now Sacramento. In January 1848, a carpenter named James Marshall was at Sutter's Mill, a mill for harvesting and cutting lumber. Marshall had helped to build the sawmill and was inspecting the area. As he later told the story, "My eye was caught by something shining in the bottom of the ditch . . . I reached my hand down and picked it up; it made my heart thump, for I was certain it was gold . . . Then I saw another."

As news of the discovery spread, people from many countries poured into California in search of riches. These prospectors and miners were nicknamed the Forty-niners, after the year the gold rush began. Free African-Americans were among the first to arrive. The rush also brought more than 20,000 Chinese immigrants across the Pacific Ocean to California. They found work in the mines and developed restaurants and laundries for the prospectors. The Chinese immigrants were not well

James Marshall discovered gold on the American River while at work inspecting a sawmill.

Early gold seekers used a technique called cradle rocking to search for gold. They dumped a mixture of earth and water into a sieve, then rocked it to separate out the gold.

treated by other immigrants, however, and laws were passed that prevented them from mining for gold. Instead, the resourceful Chinese people found other ways to make their fortunes in California.

California's cities boomed. Hundreds of mining camps and towns were created almost overnight, jammed with prospectors trying to stake their claims. Between 1848 and 1856, an estimated $465 million worth of gold was taken out of the rivers and mines of California. San Francisco had been a tiny settlement before the gold rush. In just one year, its population went from 5,000 people in July 1849 to 25,000 people in December. California was gaining popularity by the day.

STATEHOOD AND THE TRANSCONTINENTAL RAILROAD

California was not content to remain a territory of the United States. The people of California wanted to become a state so that they could participate fully in their government. However, there was a great deal of argument about whether California should be admitted as a slave-owning state—a state that permitted people to own African-Americans as servants. Southern states commonly allowed people to own slaves, but many new states were being admitted as free states, where slavery was not permitted. Southern leaders feared that they would lose power within the government, and they demanded that each new free state be balanced with a slave state. Finally, California was allowed to enter the United States as a free state in 1850. The city of San Jose was California's first capital. Shortly after, the capital was moved to Vallejo and again to Benicia. In 1854, the city of Sacramento grew so wealthy as a result of the gold rush that it offered a million dollars in gold for the privilege of becoming the state's new capital. Sacramento is still the capital today.

In spite of California's popularity, it was still isolated from the rest of the country. In those days, it took four or five months to travel from San Francisco to New York. People took stagecoaches or wagons, or went all the way around South America by ship. The postal service, known as the Pony Express, and the invention of the telegraph helped to link California with the rest of the country, but the best solution was a railroad. In 1862 President Abraham Lincoln signed the Pacific Railroad Act, and work on the railroad began.

Two railroad companies, the Union Pacific and the Central Pacific, worked together. Many Chinese-Americans worked on construction of the railroad, drilling and blasting their way across the United States. When the Transcontinental Railroad was finally completed seven years later in 1869, it was cause for

Chinese-Americans were the primary workers on the Transcontinental Railroad. Many risked their lives, and some died from the harsh winters and dangerous conditions.

great celebration. The new railroad linked east to west and would open up many areas of settlement.

Sadly, though the Chinese people worked long and hard to contribute to their new country, they were still excluded from society. They kept to themselves and created small communities called Chinatowns. The Chinese banded together to protect their rights and their traditions.

IMMIGRATION AND THE CIVIL WAR

The years after the gold rush brought hundreds of thousands of people to the Golden State. People from Asia, Italy, Ireland, Germany, and Russia came to settle in California during this time. Each new wave brought people with different languages, skills, and cultures. The Italians, for example, were skilled wine makers who knew how to grow special grapes for wine. Others brought olive trees and citrus fruits. California's first vineyards were planted by 1861, and the first trainload of oranges was shipped from Los Angeles in 1866.

During the 1800s, the states began arguing over slavery. Northerners wanted to abolish, or do away with, slavery. Southerners defended their tradition and said slaves were important to their economy. When Abraham Lincoln was elected president in 1860, he wanted to unite North and South and put an end to slavery. The southern states felt threatened by this. As a result, eleven southern states seceded, or separated, from the Union and formed the Confederate States of America.

Today's Chinatown in Los Angeles is full of culture, activity, and tourists, as well as more than 12,000 people who call it their home.

Tension between North and South became so great that in 1861 the Civil War (1861–1865) broke out. Confederates in the South fought against Unionists from the North. Since California had been admitted to the United States as a free state, its volunteers fought on the Union side. California provided 15,725 volunteers to the Union army, including two full regiments and one battalion. Most Californians did not fight in the east but stayed in the west to protect the Pacific Coast. California gold helped to pay for the Union effort. The war ended in April 1865, when General Robert E. Lee surrendered his Confederate troops to Union General Ulysses S. Grant in Virginia. The Union had won the war.

THE TURN OF THE CENTURY

The years following the Civil War brought tremendous growth to California. After the war ended, many free African-Americans made their way to California for a new start. Many other new settlers also wanted to make their homes in the Golden State.

California had its share of growing pains. For example, the area around San Francisco harbor came to be known as the Barbary Coast, after a famous pirate coast in Africa. This part of the city had a high crime rate. Gamblers, thieves, and other criminals lived there in great numbers. Unsuspecting immigrants and seamen were harassed and forced to give up their savings.

At the same time, there were good things happening in California. New inventions such as irrigation made it possible to pump water to farms all over California. New methods of farming and different kinds of crops made farmers richer. The California valleys became the greatest food producing area in the United States, with crops such as wheat, cotton, oranges, and lemons.

Many tourists from the United States and other countries thought that California's mild climate was good for their health. Often they came just for a visit, and decided to stay. With all the people coming into the state, more homes were needed. Lots of houses and other buildings were built all over California.

It was in the midst of this good fortune that tragedy occurred. On April 18, 1906, San Francisco was rocked by an earthquake that lasted just over a minute. People poured into the streets as buildings collapsed. Streets and sidewalks buckled and heaved beneath their feet. The earthquake caused terrible damage, but even worse were the fires that raged through the city afterward. Many homes were lit by gas and kerosene, which only added fuel to the fires. In the end, about 3,000 people died. Californians have

Oakland was one of many cities that grew rapidly in the early 1900s. City Hall, pictured here, was America's first high-rise government building.

The 1906 earthquake and resulting fires destroyed much of San Francisco. Many buildings had to be blasted with dynamite in order to control the raging fires.

since learned their lesson from this tragedy. Laws were passed that required strict building codes to make sure that new houses and other buildings were strong enough to withstand another earthquake.

In the early 1900s, Southern California was shaken up once again—this time by the invention of the movie camera. Thomas Edison invented the movie camera, which gave birth to a whole new art form—moving pictures, or "movies" for short. People poured into a place called Hollywood, located on the outskirts of Los Angeles. They wanted to make movies, see movies, and star in movies. Early filmmakers liked California because there was such a huge variety of scenery there. They could film everything from westerns to snowstorms to beach scenes, all within a short distance of each other. People couldn't seem to get enough of the movies, and movie studios were filming as many as twenty movies a week. The film industry that grew up in Hollywood has had a major impact on people and culture all over the world.

Californians were brought into fighting once again during World War I (1914–

EXTRA! EXTRA!

One of the first movies ever made was called *The Great Train Robbery*, made in 1903. It was filmed in black and white, and none of the actors had any speaking parts—it was a silent movie! Even without words (or color), it was a smashing success. *The Great Train Robbery* was based on real train robberies of that time period and was the first movie that could be called a western.

1918), or "the war to end all wars." The United States was at war with Germany, and fighting went on in Europe and elsewhere. California's position near the Pacific Ocean meant that a strong navy force was needed to defend American shores. At the same time many Californians joined the army and were sent to Europe. Among the most famous of these soldiers was the great movie actor and comedian Buster Keaton. Keaton once said that his army uniform was much too big and that he had to wear boots that were two sizes too big!

The end of World War I and the 1920s brought a period of good times to Americans. Sometimes called the Roaring Twenties, these years brought tremendous growth to California. Automobiles took the place of horses and wagons. Cities such as Los Angeles became even bigger and more spread out, because automobiles made traveling faster and easier. Highways were built to connect states and cities. Silent films gave way to "talkies," or movies with sound. It may have seemed like the good times would last forever, but by the end of the decade everything would change.

THE GREAT DEPRESSION AND ANOTHER WORLD WAR

October 1929 began a period known as the Great Depression. The economy in America and all over the world suffered greatly. The value of many goods was suddenly almost nothing. Banks closed, and thousands of people lost their jobs and even their homes.

During the 1930s, several years of terrible drought plagued the central United States. The earth was dry and dusty, layers of topsoil blew away, and the area became known as the Dust Bowl. Many farmers from Kansas, Texas, and Oklahoma, unable to grow crops or make a living, gave up their farms and moved west to

To escape the dust and heat, many families packed their belongings into covered wagons and headed to California from Oklahoma, Kansas, and Texas.

California. They moved from one farm to another, helping to harvest California's crops. Many Mexicans also came to California during these years, looking for work and a better life. Between 1934 and 1940, almost 400,000 people poured into California. Most of these people were very poor, and crime and conflict were often the result of frustration and overcrowded living conditions.

The Great Depression gradually ended after World War II (1939–1945) began. As the United States prepared to go to war with Europe, manufactured goods were once again in demand. People found jobs in factories and made enough money to buy homes, food, and clothing. Even the movies were in demand, but for a different reason. The United States Army asked Hollywood to create short films about the U.S. military for public viewing. Also, many branches of the military were growing at a fast pace. They wanted films to show recruits, or new soldiers, that would help to train them. The First Motion Picture Unit of the U.S. Army Air Force was set in motion.

California played an important role in World War II. Not only was California an important point for defending American shores, it was also the place where ships, soldiers, and supplies traveled to support the war in the Pacific. Military installations and training camps were built all over the state. Fort Ord, near Monterey, was one of the largest. California's geography was also advantageous. The military could train soldiers to

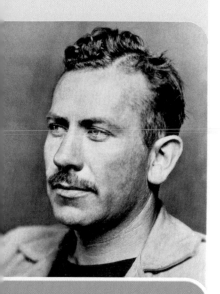

fight on all kinds of terrain—deserts, snow, and forests—and in different climates. Because of this training, soldiers were better able to fight in different countries.

But the war years brought problems, too. Because the United States was at war with Japan, many people lost trust in the Japanese. They feared that Japanese-Americans would be loyal to Japan and not the United States. More than 100,000 Americans of Japanese descent were rounded up and sent to camps such as Manzanar and Tule Lake. These people lost their homes and businesses and were forced to live in bad conditions at the camps. At the same time, however, there were many Japanese-American soldiers who fought bravely for the United States.

Thousands of Japanese-Americans were held prisoner in camps at Manzanar, in Owens Valley.

GROWING PAINS

After the war ended in 1945, prosperity led to even more rapid population growth in California. Many African-Americans came to the state to work in factories during the war and stayed there when the war was over. However, many people did not see African-Americans as equal to whites. They were treated unfairly and discriminated against throughout the United States, as well as in California. Jim Crow laws were passed, creating segregation, or separation, of whites from blacks. African-Americans had to sit in special places on buses and trains. African-American children couldn't even attend the same schools as whites.

In 1954 the Supreme Court passed a law that made segregated schools illegal. Schools were forced to allow African-American children to go to school with white children. This was an important time for African-Americans, but there was still a long way to go. They wanted equal rights and equal pay.

In 1964 Californians voted in favor of a law that allowed discrimination against African-Americans in real estate dealings. Shortly after, during the summer of 1965, riots broke out in an African-American section of Los Angeles called Watts. People

Fire trucks tackled burning buildings during the Watts riot, which left 34 people dead.

robbed homes and businesses and burned local stores. During the six days of the riots, thirty-four people died.

During the 1960s, migrant farm workers formed a union under the leadership of a man named Cesar Chavez. Migrant farm workers moved from farm to farm in California, helping to harvest the state's crops. Although they were important to California's economy, they were often not given fair treatment. The union helped to make sure the migrant workers got fair wages and benefits. Chavez organized a strike, and the union members refused to work. Crops spoiled because there was no one to pick them. Finally, employers agreed to fair pay and benefits, and the strike was settled.

The 1960s were also a time of change for America's young people. They had revolutionary ideas about education, lifestyles, and laws. College students in California protested the Vietnam War (1964–1973) and promoted civil rights. In San Francisco, thousands of young people were drawn to the Haight-Ashbury district, known for its diverse cultural background. These "hippies" or "flower children" experimented with peaceful demonstrations. A whole new generation of American music, performed by such stars as Jimi Hendrix and Janis Joplin, made these new ideas even more popular.

In the 1970s and 1980s, California continued to grow rapidly. During this time many people were drawn to the Central Valley rather than the coastal cities. As a result, cities such as Riverside, San Bernardino, Modesto, Stockton, Bakersfield, and Sacramento were among the fastest-growing in the nation. More and more people came to the state to work in new industries such as computers and other types of technology. This era saw the beginning of what has become known as Silicon Valley. In the 1970's, Steven Jobs and Stephen Wozniak formed Apple Computer Inc., and a whole new industry was born.

Steven Jobs formed Apple Computer, Inc., a company known for being at the forefront of computer technology.

A Los Angeles apartment building collapsed onto the garage below during an earthquake in 1994.

RECENT TIMES

The year 1989 brought another major earthquake to the San Francisco-Oakland area. A long section of the San Francisco-Oakland Bay Bridge collapsed. The early 1990s saw periods of heavy flooding in the northern part of California, while in the south, droughts led to conditions that enabled brush fires to spread. Scientists believe that these conditions were caused by changes in the upper air currents over the Pacific Ocean.

During the 1990s, California had its share of social problems. Just as there were great contrasts in the weather, there were great contrasts in the lives of Californians. Many people struck it rich in the computer, entertainment, and technology industries, but other people lost their jobs and were unemployed. It seemed like the rich were getting richer and the poor were getting poorer. Since the state was so heavily populated, the state government had to work hard to come up with new ways to solve these problems. California was one of the first states to start programs to train unemployed people for

new jobs. The government helped send them to schools where they learned new skills in different industries. In this way it was possible for many people to change careers.

Racial tensions also broke out again. Four Los Angeles policemen brutally beat an African-American motorist, Rodney King. Though the police had stopped his car for a traffic violation, they believed King to be violent. A videotape of the event showed that police used too much force, but the officers were acquitted at their trial. This decision by the courts led to protests, riots, and demonstrations against police brutality all over the country.

During this period, Californians became increasingly concerned about the environment. Air pollution is a big problem in California's cities, and laws were passed to make sure that automobiles did not contribute to the problem. These efforts led to new air-pollution laws and standards all over America. Efforts to clean up and protect the ocean have also met with great success.

The Los Angeles riot of 1992 was the worst in United States history.

Water continues to be a big problem for Californians. Pumps bring water to dry areas of the state, but California's huge population sometimes means there's not enough water to go around. Most of the water is in the northern part of the state, but most of the people are in the south. Water conservation is very important to Californians. New efforts are being made to find ways to remove the salt from seawater and use the water for other purposes.

A huge crisis for California came in 2001, when energy became too expensive for people to afford. At the time, 600,000 new residents were moving into the state every year, but not enough new power plants were being built. Also, very hot summers and cold winters had created an especially big demand for energy. In January 2001, rolling blackouts took place in some parts of the state, and power was turned off for thousands of people for an hour at a time. If this situation continues, energy losses could also hurt California's crops, particularly oranges. Electricity is needed for fans and water pumps that help to warm orange groves when it is cold. The state and federal governments are working together to find a solution to California's energy crisis.

In spite of these problems, the future looks bright for California. Every day, people are finding new ways to protect their state's precious natural resources while maintaining growth. California is also pioneering new forms of energy, such as solar energy, and even using garbage as fuel. Californians are facing the future with the same sense of hope and adventure that the first settlers brought to this beautiful "paradise on the Pacific."

FIND OUT MORE

California is taking steps to protect children from air pollution, or the contamination of air by harmful substances. Children breathe about twice as often as adults, and so they breathe in twice as much polluted air. What are some things that might cause air pollution?

43

CHAPTER FOUR

GOVERNING CALIFORNIA

The domed ceiling inside the capitol building is an impressive sight.

California's state constitution, a document that defines how the state will be governed, was adopted in 1849. Throughout history, changes, or amendments, were made to the original document, and today's constitution was adopted in 1879. The constitution gives Californians the right to vote for or against changes in their state's laws. They can also vote to add laws and to remove from office elected officials who aren't doing a good job. Since 1879 Californians have made hundreds of changes to their state constitution.

California's state government is set up like the federal government. There are three branches of government—the executive, the legislative, and the judicial. Together, these branches of government make and carry out laws that protect the welfare of all citizens. No single branch has more power than another, which provides a balance of power within the state government.

The executive branch enforces and carries out the state's laws. The head of the executive branch is the governor, who is elected by the people of California. After being elected, he or she serves a four-year term in office. No governor can serve more than two terms, or eight years. The governor plays a role in deciding how much money the state will spend on things like highways and schools. He or she also appoints other important people in the state government, like the state director of health services. The governor cannot make laws, but can veto, or say no to, laws proposed by the legislative branch. The governor is also commander-in-chief of California's military and can call them into action to protect the people of California in an emergency.

The lieutenant governor is second in line after the governor. He or she is elected separately. The lieutenant governor's responsibilities

Visitors can tour the state capitol and watch the legislature in session.

45

FIND OUT MORE

An idea for a new law is called a bill. Bills can start off with one person's idea, or maybe that of a group of people. If you had an idea for a new California law, who would you need to talk to in the government?

include creating jobs for the state, protecting California's environment, and improving schools.

THE LEGISLATIVE BRANCH

The legislative branch makes laws for the state. This branch is made up of a state senate and a state assembly. California is divided into forty voting districts that are determined by the number of people who live in a particular area. For example, Southern California has a larger population than Northern California, so it has more voting districts. Each senator and assembly member represents one of these districts.

There are forty senators for the state of California, and eighty members of the assembly. Assembly members are elected every two years and can serve up to three terms in office. Senators are elected every four years and can serve no more than two terms in office.

If you tour the capitol building at the right time you can watch the Senate in session.

THE JUDICIAL BRANCH

The judicial branch interprets California's laws and resolves disputes, or disagreements, concerning the law. California's court system is made up of two kinds of courts—trial courts, also known as superior courts, and appellate courts, which includes the Supreme Court. In a trial court, a judge and sometimes a jury listen to the facts of a case. After hearing from both sides, the court makes a decision in favor of one side or the other. Trial courts hear many kinds of cases, including those that involve young people and cases that involve money damages of $5,000 or less. Each of the 58 counties in California has its own superior court. Superior court judges serve six-year terms.

If people are not satisfied with the decision of the trial court, they can make an appeal, or present their case again to a higher court—the court of appeals. The court of appeals determines if the lower court made a mistake in its decision. After the court of appeals a case can still be brought to the Supreme Court, California's highest court.

The Supreme Court is where cases and issues that cannot be settled elsewhere are decided. A state Supreme Court decision can be overturned only by the United States Supreme Court, which is the highest court in the country. California's Supreme Court is made up of a chief justice, or judge, and six associate justices, who are appointed by the governor. Each justice serves twelve years on the Supreme Court.

WHO'S WHO IN CALIFORNIA?

Earl Warren (1891–1974) of Los Angeles was appointed the fourteenth Chief Justice of the United States Supreme Court in 1953. An important decision made by his court was that racial segregation is unconstitutional. Earl Warren College at the University of California, San Diego was named in his honor.

CALIFORNIA STATE GOVERNMENT

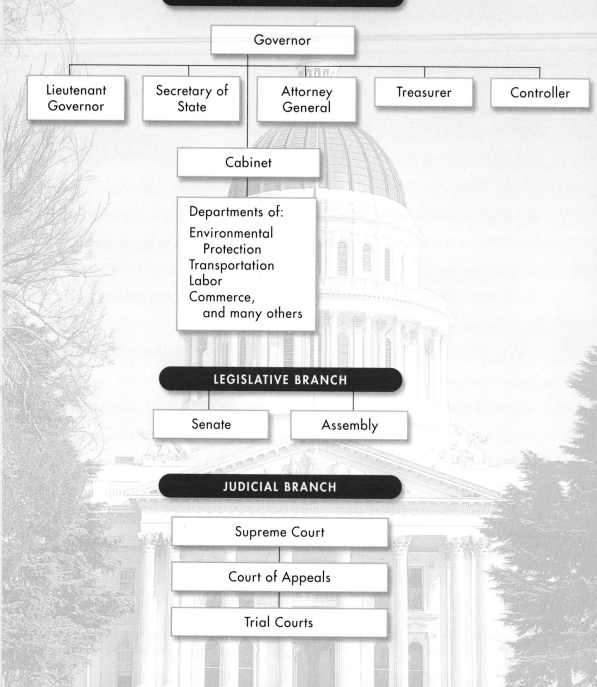

EXECUTIVE BRANCH

Governor

Lieutenant Governor

Secretary of State

Attorney General

Treasurer

Controller

Cabinet

Departments of:

Environmental Protection
Transportation
Labor
Commerce,
 and many others

LEGISLATIVE BRANCH

Senate

Assembly

JUDICIAL BRANCH

Supreme Court

Court of Appeals

Trial Courts

CALIFORNIA GOVERNORS

Name	Term	Name	Term
Peter H. Burnett	1849–1851	James Herbert Budd	1895–1899
John McDougal	1851–1852	Henry T. Gage	1899–1903
John Bigler	1852–1856	Dr. George C. Pardee	1903–1907
John Neely Johnson	1856–1858	James Norris Gillett	1907–1911
John B. Weller	1858–1860	Hiram Warren Johnson	1911–1917
Milton Slocum Latham	1860–1860 (5 days)	William Dennison Stephens	1917–1923
		Friend William Richardson	1923–1927
John G. Downey	1860–1862	Clement C. Young	1927–1931
Leland Stanford	1862–1863	James Rolph, Jr.	1931–1934
Frederick F. Low	1863–1867	Frank F. Merriam	1934–1939
Henry H. Haight	1867–1871	Culbert Levy Olson	1939–1943
Newton Booth	1871–1875	Earl F. Warren	1943–1953
Romualdo Pacheco	1875–1875	Goodwin J. Knight	1953–1959
William Irwin	1875–1880	Edmund G. Brown	1959–1967
George Clement Perkins	1880–1883	Ronald Wilson Reagan	1967–1975
George B. Stoneman	1883–1887	Edmund G. Brown, Jr.	1975–1983
Washington Bartlett	1887–1887	George Deukmejian	1983–1991
Robert W. Waterman	1887–1891	Pete Wilson	1991–1999
Henry H. Markham	1891–1895	Gray Davis	1999–

Sacramento was founded by John Sutter, Jr. He was the son of John Sutter, who owned the sawmill where gold was first discovered in California. In 1854 Sacramento became the state capital.

Sacramento is in a wonderful location. The city is located at the point where the American and Sacramento rivers come together. Nestled between the Sierra Mountains to the east and the Coastal Ranges to the west, Sacramento sits in the center of some of the most beautiful scenery in the world. With a population of about 400,000 people, Sacramento is the largest inland city in the northern part of the state. It is the seventh largest city in California.

The capitol building was completed in 1874. At the top of the building is a glass dome that reaches 210 feet (64 m) above the street. When it was first built, the builders included real California gold in the dome. The building was restored in 1971, when an earthquake hit Sacramento. Although the quake didn't damage the capitol, the government decided to restore the building, making it strong enough to resist future earthquakes. Today, the assembly and the senate meet in the capitol building. If you visit on the right day, you can watch the legislature in session.

The historic governor's mansion is not far from the capitol. Now a state park and museum, the mansion was home to thirteen of California's governors and their families in the early 1900s. Also nearby is the California State Railroad Museum, the largest of its kind in the United

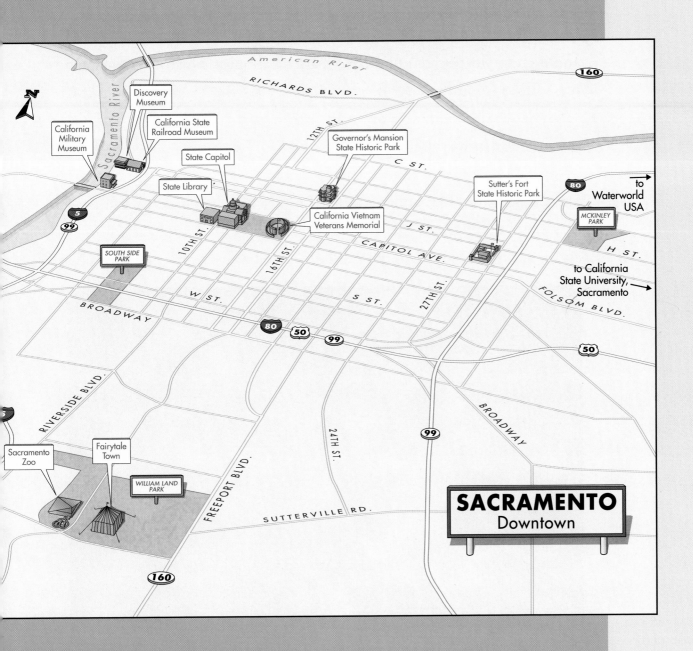

California Military Museum

Discovery Museum

California State Railroad Museum

State Capitol

State Library

Governor's Mansion State Historic Park

California Vietnam Veterans Memorial

Sutter's Fort State Historic Park

American River

RICHARDS BLVD.

Sacramento River

C ST.

J ST.

CAPITOL AVE.

12TH ST.

10TH ST.

16TH ST.

27TH ST.

SOUTH SIDE PARK

W ST.

S ST.

BROADWAY

MCKINLEY PARK

to Waterworld USA

to California State University, Sacramento

H ST.

FOLSOM BLVD.

BROADWAY

24TH ST.

99

Sacramento Zoo

Fairytale Town

WILLIAM LAND PARK

RIVERSIDE BLVD.

FREEPORT BLVD.

SUTTERVILLE RD.

SACRAMENTO
Downtown

160

States. You can step inside an old-time locomotive, watch slide shows, and even use its research library to learn all about the history of the railroad. Every June the city of Sacramento hosts the California Railroad Festival, which highlights the museum. It is the most-visited railroad museum in the world.

Sacramento began life as a fort. Today you can visit Sutter's Fort State Historical Park and see how the fort once looked. In the gold rush days, many of the city's residents were very rich, and their homes and mansions are open to the public. These homes have been carefully

The California State Railroad Museum has restored locomotives and railroad cars to illustrate the railroad history of California.

preserved and restored to their original condition. You'll also see people dressed as doctors, blacksmiths, and sailors from the 1840s. You can also learn about the famous event that made history at Sutter's Fort.

Sacramento offers plenty of places for fun, too. The Sacramento Zoo is a great place to spend a day. The zoo has more than 400 animals and offers talks and stage presentations too. You'll see all kinds of animals including Asian lions, zebras, cheetas, chimpanzees, and 53 species of reptiles. The Discovery Museum, also in Sacramento, has lots of hands-on exhibits where you can learn about history, science, and technology. At the Gold Gallery you can see a mine shaft, examine pieces of gold, and walk through old-time Sacramento to experience what it must have been like during the gold rush. Or, you can relax in the planetarium and explore the stars and planets. If you want to travel to the stars, check out the Challenger Learning Center to see how it feels to be at mission control on a space shuttle.

You can find out what life was like in 1846 by taking a trip to see Sutter's Fort, where gold was first discovered.

CHAPTER FIVE

THE PEOPLE AND PLACES OF CALIFORNIA

The Kelp Forest exhibit at Monterey Bay Aquarium is 28 feet deep and holds 335,000 gallons of water. You can watch divers hand-feed the fish.

There is wonderful variety among the people of California. With many cultural groups and traditions, Californians can be proud of their heritage. Larger numbers of Caucasian, Hispanic, and Asian people live here than in any other state. California is also home to the second-largest populations of African-American and Native American populations than any other state. More than half of the people living in California were born somewhere else, and about half of the people in that group—almost 17 out of every 100 people—were born in other countries. California is home to the largest population of Koreans, Guatemalans, Vietnamese, Armenians, and Iranians outside of their own countries.

There are many reasons people come to California. Most often, people come seeking a better way of life. Wherever they come from, each group contributes part of their culture and heritage to the life of all Californians. Almost everywhere you can find fascinating evidence of the different foods, styles of building, languages, types of music, and arts that people from all over the world have brought to the Golden State. In Los Angeles County alone, there are eighty languages spoken in the public school system and more than fifty foreign-language newspapers.

WORKING IN CALIFORNIA

The jobs and careers of Californians are as varied and interesting as the types of people who live there. Because of the rich lands and mild climate, farming is important to the state. California is one of the top agriculture states in the country. Many people are farmers or work on farms, tending such varied crops as grapes, citrus, all sorts of vegetables, nuts, and berries. There are even flower farms in California. These farms supply flower shops all over the country. If you send someone flowers for a

Pottery classes, basket weaving, and traditional dancing are just a few of the activities that take place at the Indian Heritage Festival in Palm Springs every year.

This flower farm in Santa Paula grows zinnias for Burpee, a popular seed and plant company.

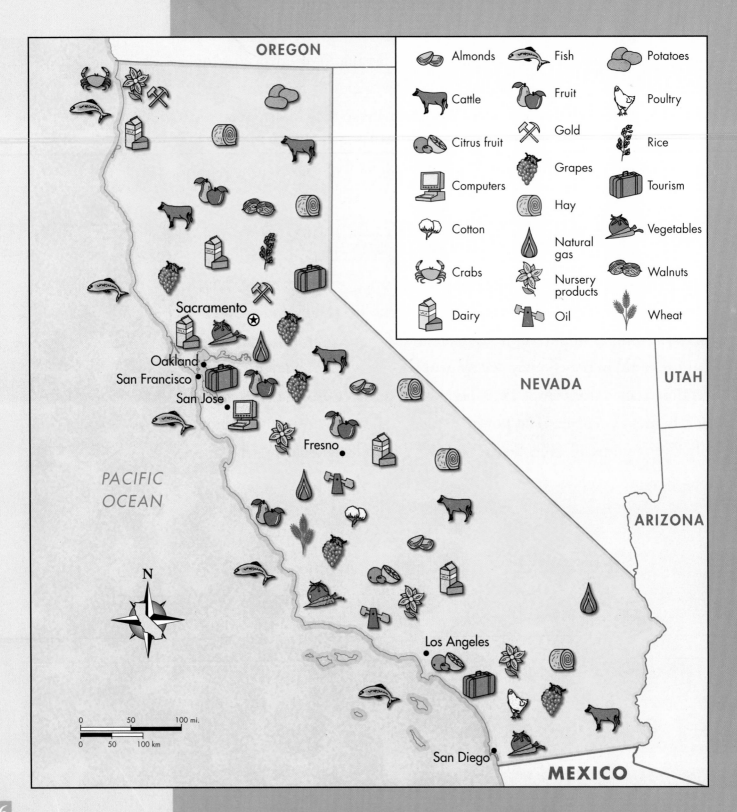

OREGON

PACIFIC OCEAN

NEVADA

UTAH

ARIZONA

MEXICO

Sacramento

Oakland
San Francisco
San Jose

Fresno

Los Angeles

San Diego

N

0   50   100 mi.

0   50   100 km

Almonds

Cattle

Citrus fruit

Computers

Cotton

Crabs

Dairy

Fish

Fruit

Gold

Grapes

Hay

Natural gas

Nursery products

Oil

Potatoes

Poultry

Rice

Tourism

Vegetables

Walnuts

Wheat

special occasion, it's likely that the flowers were grown in California. More than 400,000 Californians earn their living by farming.

Manufacturing, or making products, is also important in California. Workers build cars, airplanes, spacecraft, and boats. Silicon Valley is famous around the world for being an important center for computer manufacturing and development. Companies such as Sun Microsystems, Hewlett Packard, and Cisco, all based in Silicon Valley, are producing ideas and products that are at the forefront of today's computer industry. Most likely, the hardware or software on your computer at school and at home was developed or made in California. Today, about 2.5 million Californians work in factories.

The Golden State is rich in natural resources. As a result, many people work in natural-gas production, mining, or the oil industry. Most people don't realize it, but there is still gold mined in California. The state ranks third in oil production in the United States. A mineral called boron, an ingredient used in soaps and medicines, is also mined in the desert areas of the state. California is the only place boron is found in North America.

Its location near the Pacific makes California an ideal place for those who earn their living fishing. As a matter of fact, California is one of the top five seafood-producing states in America. Tuna, sardines, swordfish, halibut, and some shellfish are all among the "catch of the day" for California fishers. If you look in your kitchen cupboard and find canned tuna or salmon, it may have been caught in the waters off the California

EXTRA! EXTRA!

California is the largest producer of *processed* tomatoes in the United States. Processed tomatoes are used for canning and to make sauces. They are put into cans less than six hours after picking. In contrast, Florida has the largest *fresh* tomato industry in the country, which means they are picked when still green and sold to stores.

From San Diego in the south to Crescent City in the north, commercial fishing produces jobs for many people along the California coast.

coast. The fishing industry creates many jobs for fish handlers and boat builders as well.

Finally, California is a good place to live if you work for the government. There are several military bases in California. State and federal governments employ almost two million workers. Edwards Air Force Base, in Southern California, is a leader in the field of developing and testing aircraft. Many important events in flight history have taken place at Edwards.

TAKE A TOUR OF CALIFORNIA

Northern California

The city of Eureka is one of the northernmost cities in California. The founder of the city, James Talbot Ryan, expressed triumph upon discovering Humboldt Bay and cried "Eureka!" (Eureka is the Greek word for

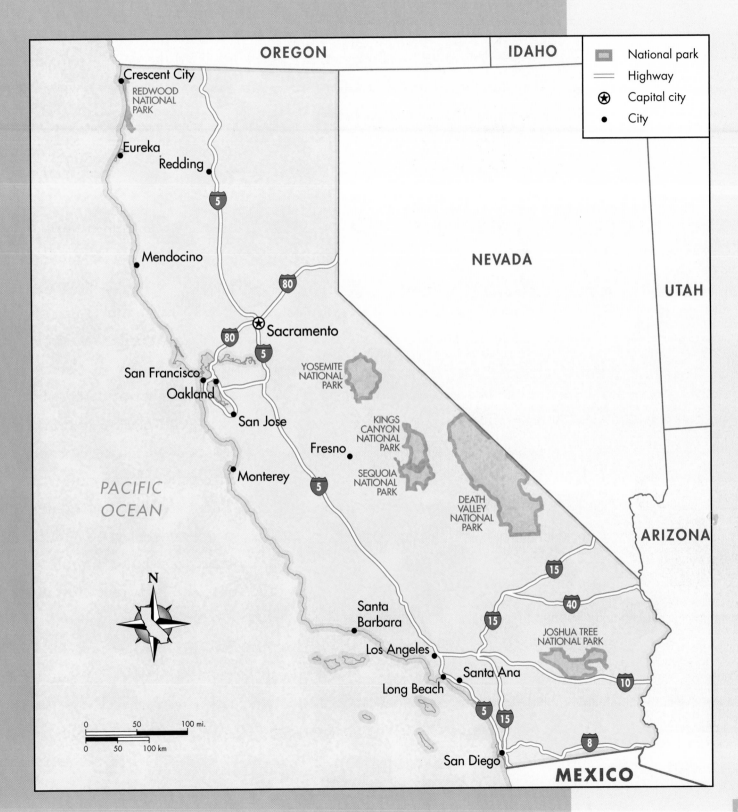

OREGON

IDAHO

National park

Highway

Capital city

City

Crescent City

REDWOOD
NATIONAL
PARK

Eureka

Redding

5

NEVADA

UTAH

Mendocino

80

80

Sacramento

5

San Francisco

Oakland

YOSEMITE
NATIONAL
PARK

San Jose

KINGS
CANYON
NATIONAL
PARK

Fresno

Monterey

SEQUOIA
NATIONAL
PARK

5

PACIFIC
OCEAN

DEATH
VALLEY
NATIONAL
PARK

ARIZONA

15

N

40

Santa
Barbara

15

JOSHUA TREE
NATIONAL
PARK

Los Angeles

Santa Ana

10

Long Beach

5

15

0   50   100 mi.

8

0   50   100 km

San Diego

MEXICO

"I have found it!") California's first legislature liked the saying so much they adopted "Eureka" as California's state motto.

Eureka is a natural deep-water port located along the northern California coast. Lumber mills were central to Eureka's early days. By 1881, over twenty sawmills processed lumber from northern California's rich forests. Eureka has more than fifty acres of redwood trees.

In the center of the city lies Old Town, where you'll find beautiful Victorian houses that were built by the city's wealthiest residents. Agate Beach is a favorite area for rock collectors, who search the shores for semiprecious stones such as carnelians. Whale watching is also a favorite pastime during the summer and fall.

Another stop in northern California is Lassen Volcanic National Park. Lassen Peak, an active volcano, erupted for the first time in 1914. There are plenty of hiking trails, so you can get a good look at the volcano as well as bubbling mud pots, a coldwater boiling lake, and wildflowers galore. If you're not into hiking, you could take the car along the 35-mile main park road to check out the

Gray whales were once close to extinction. Today there are more than 20,000 gray whales in the Pacific Ocean.

Guacamole is a popular dip that is often served with corn chips or tortillas. This recipe uses the best fresh produce and reflects California's Mexican heritage. Remember to ask an adult to help with the chopping!

CALIFORNIA GUACAMOLE

1 ripe avocado, peeled and pitted
1 medium tomato, chopped
2 green onions, chopped
1 tablespoon mayonnaise
juice of one lemon
a dash of hot sauce
chopped fresh cilantro leaves

1. In a medium-size bowl, mash the avocado with a fork until it is fairly smooth.
2. Add the chopped tomato, onions, mayonnaise, lemon juice and seasonings.
3. Mix until almost smooth. Chill before serving.

Lassen Peak stood out as a landmark for people traveling west in the mid-1800s.

scenery. In the wintertime, snowshoeing and sledding are popular activities at the park.

Lake Tahoe is a popular vacation destination all year round. In the spring you can go hot-air ballooning, golfing, and mountain-biking. In the winter it's a great place to ski and snowboard. There are 28 skiing areas with some of the steepest, most scenic runs in the west.

Central California

The most-visited place in central California is San Francisco. Nicknamed the City by the Bay, San Francisco is marked by rolling hills, beautiful parks, and grand Victorian homes. There are lots of interest-

ing things to see and do in San Francisco. Fisherman's Wharf is a place that used to house fish markets and factories but now has restaurants and shops, as well as Ripley's Believe It Or Not Museum. Beautiful Golden Gate Park was built on sand dunes but is now a lush green refuge in the heart of the city. The famous conservatory in the park is home to some rare and endangered species of plants and flowers. The Golden Gate Bridge is also located here and is considered to be a masterpiece of engineering.

San Francisco is well known for its many steep hills and crooked streets. Lombard Street is famous for being "the crookedest street in the world." A good way to travel San Francisco's steep hills is on a cable car.

This famous row of restored Victorian homes is often referred to as the Seven Sisters.

To travel down Lombard Street by car you'd better have good brakes and a lot of patience!

Cable cars were invented in 1867 by Andrew Hallidie. After seeing a terrible horse-and-wagon accident, he wanted to come up with a safer way to travel. Cable cars are pulled along an underground cable as the car travels up and down steep hills and winding tracks. Today, each cable car has three brakes that are operated by hand. The men who run the cars are called gripmen.

EXTRA! EXTRA!

One of the top tourist attractions in San Francisco is Alcatraz Island. The building on Alcatraz was used as a federal prison from 1934 to 1963. During that time, many prison guards lived on the island with their wives and children, who took the ferry back and forth to school on the mainland. Today you can take a tour of the prison.

After the cable car was invented, many other cities began using them. Today San Francisco is the last city in the world that still operates cable cars.

Also in central California is the city of San Jose, founded in 1777. San Jose was the first town in California that did not begin as a mission settlement. Today it is the third-largest city in California. It is in the Santa Clara Valley, an area that is nicknamed Silicon Valley. This valley is the center of a multibillion-dollar computer hardware and software industry.

EXTRA! EXTRA!

In San Jose you can visit one of the strangest museums in the world—the Winchester Mystery House. The Winchester house was built by Sarah Winchester in 1884. It has 160 rooms, 3 working elevators, and 47 fireplaces. It also has stairways that lead nowhere and doors that open up to blank walls. Sarah asked for so many additions that carpenters worked on the house twenty-four hours a day for 38 years.

Yosemite National Park is also in central California, in the Sierra Nevada. In addition to impressive waterfalls and interesting rock formations, Yosemite is the home of the giant sequoia trees. Giant sequoias are the largest living things on earth and are considered a national treasure. Yosemite is also a great place to spot all kinds of animals, including mule deer, the Sierra black bear, and more than 220 species of birds.

Southern California

Los Angeles is one of the most popular places to visit in southern California. There are various parts of Los Angeles, which are connected by a very busy freeway system. El Barrios in east Los Angeles is home to a large Mexican-American community. Many African-Americans live in south-central Los Angeles.

This area of downtown Los Angeles has been restored to look like a village in old Mexico.

The Legends of Holly-
wood mural spans the side
of a building along Hollywood Boulevard. Marilyn
Monroe, Humphrey Bogart,
and Fred Astaire, shown
here, were all popular
Hollywood stars.

Los Angeles is a very glamorous city that offers visitors a lot to see and do. You can take a tour of Universal Studios, the world's largest movie and television studio. You could also walk down Hollywood Boulevard and count the "stars" on the Walk of Fame or go shopping with the rich and famous along Rodeo Drive. Don't forget about Disneyland in nearby Anaheim!

If you're in the mood for museum-hopping, check out Exposition Park downtown. Here you'll find three museums—the California Science Center, the California African American Museum, and the Natural History Museum. The Griffith Park Observatory is another major tourist attraction, where you can visit the astronomy museum and look through telescopes. There's also a Laserium show that uses a combination of music and laser lights.

FIND OUT MORE

It isn't often that a newborn baby makes history—unless it's part of an endangered species! In 1999 Hua Mei, a giant panda cub, was born at the San Diego Zoo with much celebration. Hua Mei is the first panda born in the Western Hemisphere in ten years. Pandas are just one of many groups of animals that are on the brink of extinction, which means that they are in danger of being wiped out completely. What other animals can you think of that are almost extinct? What can we do to save them?

At the San Diego Zoo you'll get a close-up view of animals in their natural habitat.

Finally, Los Angeles is home to some very popular sports teams. Dodger Stadium is home to the L.A. Dodgers baseball team, which has won the World Series a number of times. The L.A. Lakers is one of the highest-ranked basketball teams in the country.

In the southwest corner of the state, the city of San Diego is the second-largest city in California. It's known as the birthplace of California because it is where Father Junipero Serra founded the first mission settlement, in 1769. A museum here is dedicated to Father Serra, where visitors can get a glimpse of what life was like in the early days of the missions.

Another attraction is the world-famous San Diego Zoo, one of the largest zoos anywhere. You'll see hundreds of animals including some of the world's rarest wildlife, like giant pandas and koalas. Zoo officials take an active interest in mating and breeding endangered species. The warm and sunny climate makes it possible to keep many kinds of animals here that might not survive in colder climates.

San Diego's beaches are also a welcome spot for visitors. You can watch surfers catching the waves or wander along the boardwalks, a favorite spot for street performers. The city is only sixteen miles from the Mexican border. San Diego's sunny climate, appealing beaches, and significance in the history of the Golden State make it an attractive destination for vacationers all over the world.

Tony Gwynn has played for the San Diego Padres for 20 seasons. He is one of 24 players in the 3,000 hit club.

CALIFORNIA ALMANAC

Statehood date and number:
September 9, 1850, 31st

State seal: Adopted 1850

State flag: Adopted 1911

Geographic center: In the San Joaquin Valley, 35 miles northeast of Medera

Total area/rank: 158,869 sq mi (411,469 sq km)/3rd

Coastline: 1,200 miles (1,931 km)

Borders: Mexico, Oregon, Nevada, Arizona, and the Pacific Ocean

Latitude and longitude: California is located approximately between 32° 30' and 42° 00' N and 114° 00' and 124° 29' W

Highest/lowest elevation: 14,494 ft (4,418 m), Mount Whitney/282 ft (86 m) below sea level in Death Valley

Hottest/coldest temperature: 134°F (57°C) at Death Valley on July 10, 1913/-45°F (-43°C) at Boca on January 20, 1937

Land area/rank: 155,973 sq mi (403,968 sq km)/3rd

Inland water area: 2,896 sq mi (7,501 sq km)/8th

Population/rank: 33,871,648/1st

Population of major cities:

Los Angeles: 3,694,820

San Diego: 1,223,400

San Jose: 894,943

San Francisco: 776,733

Long Beach: 461,522

Fresno: 427,652

Sacramento: 407,018

Origin of state name: California, after a mythical paradise

State capital: Sacramento

Previous capitals: San Jose, Vallejo, and Benicia

Counties: 58

State government: 40 senators, 80 representatives

Major rivers, lakes: Sacramento, San Joaquin, Colorado, Pit, Feather, Yuba, American, Stanislaus, Merced, Kings, Mokelumne, Lake Tahoe, Clear Lake, Salton Sea, Mono Lake, Shasta Lake

Farm products: Tomatoes, almonds, apricots, avocados, artichokes, broccoli, Brussels sprouts, dates, figs, garlic, nectarines, olives, peaches, plums, melons, persimmons, pomegranates, walnuts, dairy products

Livestock: Cattle/calves, sheep/lambs, hogs/pigs, chickens

Manufactured products: Food processing, transportation equipment, electrical and electronic equipment, paper, fiber, cement, clothing, fabricated metals

Mining products: Petroleum, natural gas, sand and gravel, boron, gold

Bird: California quail
Flower: California poppy
Motto: "Eureka"
Nickname: The Golden State
Song: "I Love You, California"
Tree: Giant redwood
Wildlife: Rattlesnakes, antelopes, squirrels, chipmunks, jack rabbits, blacktailed deer, skunks, bobcats, weasels, ringtailed wildcats, mountain lions, coyotes, wolverines, cougars, pelicans, wood ducks, mallards, hawks, owls

Fishing products: Striped bass, perch, steelhead and rainbow trout, salmon, sturgeon, red snapper, squid, tuna, clams, mackerel
Animal: Grizzly bear
Artifact: Carved stone bear

TIMELINE

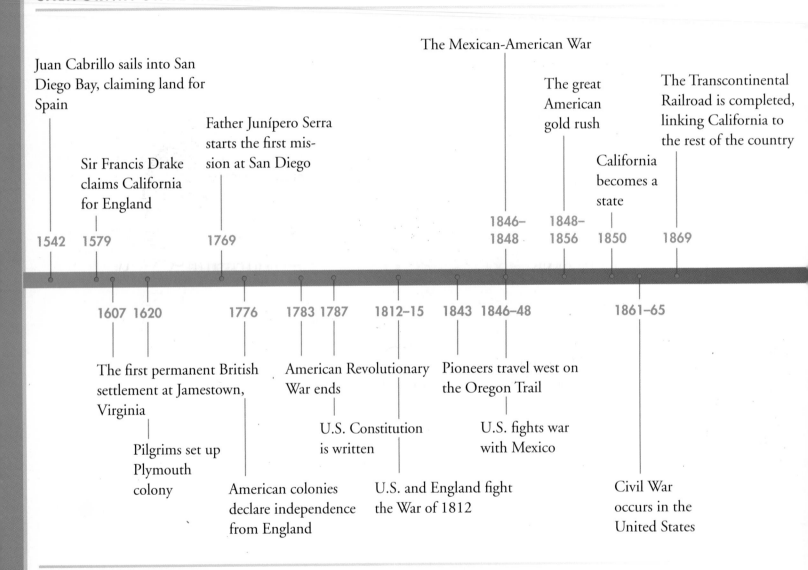

The Mexican-American War

Juan Cabrillo sails into San Diego Bay, claiming land for Spain

The great American gold rush

The Transcontinental Railroad is completed, linking California to the rest of the country

Father Junípero Serra starts the first mission at San Diego

Sir Francis Drake claims California for England

California becomes a state

1542   **1579**

1769

1846–1848   **1848–1856**   **1850**   **1869**

1607 1620   **1776**   **1783 1787**   **1812–15**   **1843 1846–48**   **1861–65**

The first permanent British settlement at Jamestown, Virginia

American Revolutionary War ends

Pioneers travel west on the Oregon Trail

Pilgrims set up Plymouth colony

U.S. Constitution is written

U.S. fights war with Mexico

American colonies declare independence from England

U.S. and England fight the War of 1812

Civil War occurs in the United States

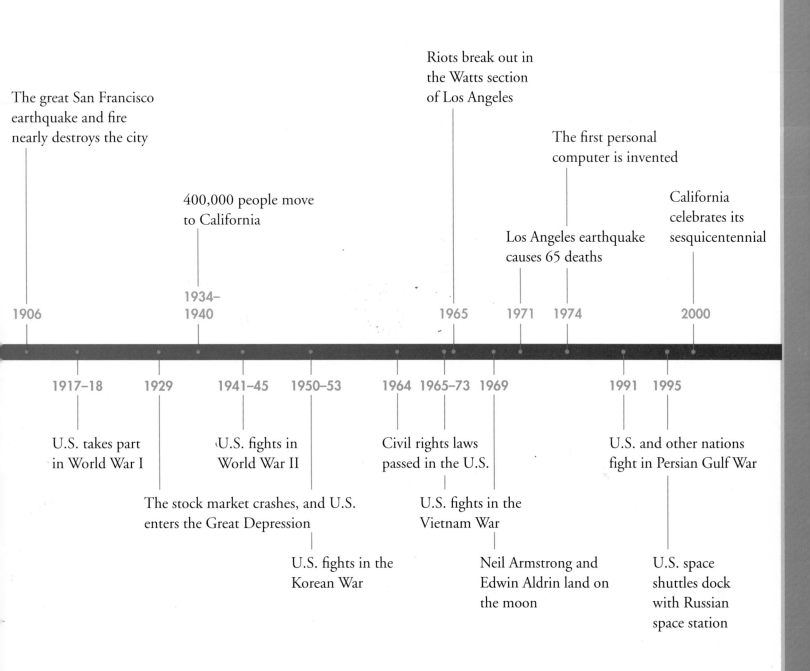

The great San Francisco earthquake and fire nearly destroys the city

Riots break out in the Watts section of Los Angeles

The first personal computer is invented

California celebrates its sesquicentennial

400,000 people move to California

Los Angeles earthquake causes 65 deaths

1906

1934– 1940

1965

1971

1974

2000

1917–18

1929

1941–45

1950–53

1964

1965–73

1969

1991

1995

U.S. takes part in World War I

U.S. fights in World War II

Civil rights laws passed in the U.S.

U.S. and other nations fight in Persian Gulf War

The stock market crashes, and U.S. enters the Great Depression

U.S. fights in the Vietnam War

U.S. fights in the Korean War

Neil Armstrong and Edwin Aldrin land on the moon

U.S. space shuttles dock with Russian space station

GALLERY OF FAMOUS CALIFORNIANS

Jennifer Aniston
(1969–)
Television actress in the popular sitcom, *Friends*.

Julia Child
(1912–)
Author and television personality. She has taught the fine art of French cuisine to generations of Americans.

Tom Hanks
(1956–)
Well-known film actor. Born in Concord.

William Randolph Hearst
(1863–1951)
Publisher, editor of national chain of newspapers and periodicals, including *Cosmopolitan*, *Harper's Bazaar*, and the San Francisco *Examiner*.

Jack London
(1876–1916)
Famous novelist and short-story writer. Born in San Francisco.

William Mulholland
(1855–1935)
Engineer in charge of creating the Los Angeles aqueduct, which brings water from the Owens River to much of Southern California.

Richard Nixon
(1913–1994)
37th president of the United States
(1969–1974).

Levi Strauss
(1829–1902)
Inventor of Levi's blue jeans, which he created as practical long-wearing clothing for gold miners.

Tiger Woods
(1975–)
Professional golfer. He has set 20 records and won the coveted Masters Tournament. Born in Cypress.

Kristi Yamaguchi
(1971–)
Professional ice skater. She won the gold medal in the 1992 Olympics. Born in Hayward.

GLOSSARY

artifact: an ancient piece of art or other evidence of civilization

conservatory: a greenhouse

delta: a mass of sand, mud, and earth that forms at the mouth of a river, usually in the shape of a triangle

Dust Bowl: a name for the drought-ridden plains states during the Great Depression

emigrate: to leave one country or region and settle in another

Forty-niner: a person who came to California during the gold rush

Great Depression: a name for a period of economic upheaval during the 1930s

immigrant: one who migrates from one place to another

irrigation: a system to pump water to crops or areas that don't get enough rain

lava: melted rock from inside a volcano

mythical: existing only in myths or stories

naturalist: a person who studies nature

prehistoric: ancient

san or santa: the Spanish word for a male or female saint, respectively

sesquicentennial: a 150-year anniversary

FOR MORE INFORMATION

Web sites

California Parks
http://funguide.com/usa/ca_parks
Includes a complete list of national and theme parks in California.

San Diego Zoo
http://www.sandiegozoo.org
The official website of the San Diego Zoo.

50 States.com
http://www.50states.com
A great source for information on California and the other 49 states.

Disneyland
http://disneyland.com
The official website of Disneyland.

State of California
http://www.ca.gov
The official website for California.

Books

Ancona, George. *Barrio: El Barrio de Jose*. New York, NY: Harcourt Brace, 1998.

Chambers, Catherine. *California Gold Rush*. Mahwah, NJ: Troll Assoc., 1998.

Curry, Jane Louise. *Back in the Beforetime: Tales of the California Indians*. New York, NY: Aladdin Paperbacks, 2001.

Stanley, Jerry. *Children of the Dust Bowl: The True Story of the School at Weedpatch Camp*. New York, NY: Crown Publishing, 1992.

Studio, Courtney. *Earthquake San Francisco, 1906*. Raintree/Steck Vaughn Pub., 1995.

Van Steenwyk, Elizabeth. *The California Missions*. Danbury, CT: Franklin Watts, 1998.

Addresses

California Travel and Tourism Publications
80 Willow Road
Menlo Park, CA 94025

Governor's Office
State Capitol Building
Sacramento, CA 95814

INDEX

Page numbers in *italics* indicate illustrations

African-Americans, 5, 28, 29, 32, 39, 42, 54, 66
Agate Beach, 60
agriculture, 15, 31, 55–57
airplane production, 57
air pollution, 42, 43
Alcatraz Island, 64
American River, 28, 50
Apple Computer company, 41, *41*
Asians, 5, 54
automobiles, 35–36

Barbary Coast, 32–33
beaches, *10*
Bear Flag Revolt, 26, 27, *27*
Bear Republic, 26–27
blackouts, 43
boat production, 57
boron mining, 57
bristlecone pines, 19
brush fires, 21, 41
Burpee seed and plant company, *55*

cable cars, 63–64, *65*
Cabrillo, Juan Rodríguez, 23
California Railroad Festival, 52
California Space Institute, 58
California State Railroad Museum, 50, *51*
Camino Real, 25
camps for Japanese-Americans, 38, *38*
capitol building, *45*, 50
Cascade mountain ranges, 12
central California, 62–66
Central Pacific Railroad, 30
Central Valley, 15, *15*, 21, 40
Challenger Learning Center, 53
Channel Islands National Park, *11*
Chavez, Cesar, 40
Chinatowns, 31, *31*
Chinese immigrants, 28–29, 30, *30*, 31
Cisco, 57
citrus, 15
Civil War, 32
climate, 21

coast, 9–12
Coastal ranges, 12
Colorado River, 19–20
computers and technology, 40–41, 57
Confederate States of America, 31
Conservatory, 63
constitution, 44
cotton, 15
court system, 47
crops, 15, 55

Death Valley, 16, 17, 21
de Portolá, Gaspar, 24
deserts, 16–19
Discovery Museum, 53
Disneyland, 67
Drake, Francis, 23–24, *24*
drought, 36–37
Dust Bowl, 36, *36*, 37

Earl Warren College, 47
earthquakes
    1906, 33–34, *34*
    1989, 41
    1994, *41*
    causes, 7, 9
    measuring with Richter Scale, 9
    San Andreas Fault, *8*
eastern California, 12–14
Edison, Thomas, 34
Edwards Air Force Base, 58
El Barrios, 66
El Niño, 21
energy crisis, 43
Eureka, 58, 60
executive branch, 45–46, 48
explorers, 23–24, 25
Exposition Park, 67

Farallons, 12
farmers, 36–37
farming, 15, 55–57
faults, 7, *8*, 9
First Motion Picture Unit of U.S Army Air Force, 37
Fisherman's Wharf, 63
fishing industry, 57–58

flag, 26–27
flower farming, *55, 55–56*
Fort Ord, 37
Forty-niners, 28
fossils, 19
Frémont, John Clement, *26, 26, 27*
fruits, 15

gem deposits, 19
geography, 7–14, 19, 23, 30, 37–38
Giant sequoias, *14, 66*
gold
    in capitol dome, 50
    cradle rocking, *28*
    discovering, 14, 28–29
    gold seekers, *28*
Golden Gate Bridge, *4,* 37, 63
Golden Gate Park, 63
Golden State, 4
Gold Gallery, 53
government, 44–47, *48*
governors, *49*
Governor's mansion, 50
Grant, Ulysses, 32
grapes, *7,* 31
gray whales, *60*
Great Central Valley. *See* Central Valley
Great Depression, 36, 37, *38*
Great Train Robbery, The, 34
Griffith Park Observatory, 67
Gwynn, Tony, 69, *69*

Haight-Ashbury district, 40
Hallidie, Andrew, 64
Hewlett Packard, 57
Hispanics, 5, 37, 54, 66
Hollywood, 34, *35,* 67
Hollywood Boulevard, *67*
Hopi nation, 33
Hua Mei, 68

immigrants. *See* people
independence from Mexico, 26–27
Indian Heritage Festival, *55*
industries, 40–41, 43
inventions. *See also* irrigation
    first personal computer, 41
    new methods of farming, 33
irrigation, 19–20, 33
islands, *11*–12

Japanese-Americans, 38, *38*
Jobs, Steven, 41
Joshua trees, 16, *17*
judicial branch, *47,* 48

Keaton, Buster, 34
Kelp Forest exhibit, *54*
Kern River, 20
King, Rodney, 42
Kings Canyon National Park, 14

L.A. Dodgers, 68
L.A. Lakers, 68
lakes, 20
Lake Tahoe, 20, *20,* 62
landforms, 9–19
La Niña, 21
Laserium show, 67
Lassen Peak, 12, 60, *62*
Lassen Volcanic National Park, 60, 62
Lee, Robert E., 32
legislative branch, 46, *48*
Lincoln, Abraham, 30
Lombard Street, 63–64, *64*
Los Angeles, *31,* 35–36, 66, *66*–68
Los Angeles ranges, 12
Los Angeles riot of 1992, *42*

Maidu nation, 22
manufactured goods, 37, 57
Manzanar, 38
maps
    agriculture, *56*
    downtown Sacramento, 51
    fun, 6
    political, 59
    topographical, 18
Marshall, James, 27–28, *28*
Mexican-Americans. *See* Hispanics
Mexico
    independence from Spain, 25
    land grants, 25
    settlers revolt, 26–27
military, Marine, and naval
    installations and camps, 21, 37–38, 58
    movies, 37
miners, 28
missionaries, 24
missions, 22, 24–25, 68
Mission San Juan Bautista, *22*

Mojave Desert, 16, *16*, 17
Monterey Bay Aquarium, *54*
mountain ranges, 12–14
Mount Whitney, 13, *13*, 14, 20
movie making, 34, *35*, 36
Muir, John, *14*
museums
    California African American Museum, 67
    California Science Center, 67
    Natural History Museum, 67

Napa Valley, *7*
national parks, 14
national wildlife refuge, 12
Native Americans 5, 54
    building missions, 24, 25
    earliest, 22–23
    helping Spanish, 23
    nations, 22, 23, *23*
    tensions with U.S. government, 33
natural resources, 43, 57
Nixon, Richard, 4
north coast, 9–10, 11
northern California, 9–10, 58, 60, 62

Oakland, *33*
Oakland Bridge, 41
oil industry, 57
Old Sacramento, *52*
Old Town, 60
olive trees, 31
oranges, 31
Owens Valley, 16, 19

Pacific Ocean, 7, 21
Pacific Railroad Act 1862, 30
Paiute nation, *23*
Palm Springs, *55*
people
    earliest inhabitants, 22
    explorers and pioneers, 1840s, 25, 26
    immigrants during Gold Rush, 31
    independence from Mexico, 26–27
    Italian immigrants, 31
    Native Americans, 23, *23*, 25
pictographs, *51*, *56*
pioneers, 25, 26
Planetarium, 53
Pomo nation, 22
population increases

after Civil War, 32–33
after Gold Rush, 31
after World War I, 35–36
during Gold Rush, 29
1970s-1980s, 40
in 2001, 43

racial segregation ruling, *47*
racial tension, 42
railroad, 30–31
recipe (California Guacamole), 61
reservoirs, 19, 20
Richter, Charles F., 9
Richter Scale, 9
Ride, Sally, 58
Ripley's Believe It Or Not Museum, 63
rivers, 19–20
Rodeo Drive, 67
Roosevelt, Theodore, 14
Ryan, James Talbot, 58

Sacramento, 30, 50, *51*, 52–53
Sacramento River, 19, 50
Sacramento Valley, 15
Sacramento Zoo, 53
Salinas, *38*
Salton Sea, 20
San Andreas fault, *8*, 22
San Bernadino mountains, 12
sand dunes, *16*
San Diego Bay, 21, 23
San Diego Padres, *69*
San Diego Zoo, *68*, 68–69
San Francisco, 24, 33–34, 40, 62, *63*, 64
San Francisco Bay, 19, 20–21
San Gabriel mountains, 12
San Jacinto mountains, 12
San Joaquin River, 19
San Joaquin Valley, 15
San Jose, 30, 65
Santa Ana winds, 21
Santa Barbara, 23
Santa Barbara Islands, *11*
Santa Clara Valley, 65
Santa Paula, *55*
Santa Rosa Island, *11*, 12
segregation, 39
Sequoia National Park, 13, *13*
Serra, Father Junípero, 24, 68
Seven Sisters, *63*

Sierra Nevada ranges, 12, *13*, 13–14, 20
Silicon Valley, 41, 57, 65
slavery, 29–30, 31
south coast, 9, 10–11
southern California, 21, 66, *66*
spacecraft production, 57
state prehistoric artifact, 22
Steinbeck, John, *38*
Sun Microsystems, 57
Sutter, John, 27, 50
Sutter, John Jr., 50
Sutter's Fort, *53*
Sutter's Fort State Historical monument, 52–53
Sutter's Mill, 27

tomato processing, 57
touring California, 50–54, 58–69
tourism, 10, 33
Transcontinental Railroad, 30, *30*, 31
trees
    giant, 66
    long-living, 19
Tule Lake, 38

unemployment, 41–42
Union army, 32
Union Pacific Railroad, 30
United Farm Workers of America, 40
Universal Studios, 67
University of California, San Diego, 47, 58

vineyards, *7*, 31
Vizcaíno, Sebastián, 24
volcanoes, 12, 60

Walk of Fame, 67
Warren, Earl, 47
water, 16–17, 19–20, 43
Watts riot, 39–40, *39*
weather. *See* climate
Winchester, Sarah, 65
Winchester Mystery House, *65*
wine, 7, 31
World War I, 34–35
World War II, 37–38, *38*
Wozniak, Stephen, 41

Yosemite National Park, 14, 66

MEET THE AUTHOR

Teresa Kennedy is the author of more than thirty books for adults and children. She lived in San Francisco from 1974 to 1976. Now she divides her time between New York City and the Catskill Mountains, where she runs The Catskill Colony for Writers.